Dear Fami...

What's the best way to help your child love reading?

Find good books like this one to share—and read together!

Here are some tips.

●**Take a "picture walk."** Look at all the pictures before you read. Talk about what you see.

●**Take turns.** Read to your child. Ham it up! Use different voices for different characters, and read with feeling! Then listen as your child reads to you, or explains the story in his or her own words.

●**Point out words as you read.** Help your child notice how letters and sounds go together. Point out unusual or difficult words that your child might not know. Talk about those words and what they mean.

●**Ask questions.** Stop to ask questions as you read. For example: "What do you think will happen next?" "How would you feel if that happened to you?"

●**Read every day.** Good stories are worth reading more than once! Read signs, labels, and even cereal boxes with your child. Visit the library to take out more books. And look for other JUST FOR YOU! BOOKS you and your child can share!

The Editors

For Joyous, Natalia, Niani, and all my brave girls, big and
small—and especially Mom, the bravest of them all!
—OG

To my wife, Olivia, for sharing her life with me,
and to our son, Sakai, for making us a family.
—RDB

Text copyright © 2004 by Olivia G. Ford.
Illustrations copyright © 2004 by Randy DuBurke.
Produced for Scholastic by COLOR-BRIDGE BOOKS, LLC, Brooklyn, NY
All rights reserved. Published by SCHOLASTIC INC.
JUST FOR YOU! is a trademark of Scholastic Inc.

Library of Congress Cataloging-in-Publication Data

George, Olivia.
    The bravest girls in the world / by Olivia George ; illustrated by Randy DuBurke.
        p. cm.—(Just for you! Level 3)
    Summary: In a new neighborhood, Toshi is reluctant to go out and make
friends because she is afraid of dogs.
    ISBN 0-439-56875-7
    [1. Fear—Fiction. 2. Dogs—Fiction.] I. DuBurke, Randy, ill. II. Title. III. Series.

PZ7.G29336Br 2004
[E]—dc22

                                                                    2004004766

10 9 8 7 6   08
            Printed in the U.S.A. 23 • First Scholastic Printing, April 2004

The Bravest Girls in the World

by Olivia George

Illustrated by Randy DuBurke

JUST FOR YOU!™
Level 3

Toshi was a pretty brave girl. There were lots of things she was not afraid of. She wasn't afraid to climb trees— even the tallest tree in her yard.

She was not afraid to jump into the
pool at the "Y" and swim from one end
to the other.

She wasn't afraid of scary movies on TV, either. Even her dad was afraid of those!

But Toshi was afraid of something. She was afraid of dogs. Dogs were so loud, and they looked so fierce! When they barked, you could see all their sharp teeth!

Toshi was so scared of meeting a dog that she hadn't walked down the block alone since she and her family moved to the city. And she hadn't made any friends.

When her mom and dad asked why she wouldn't go outside to play, she told them that the big kids who played jump rope outside looked mean.

But what she was really afraid of was the dogs.

Who knew how many dogs there might be on this block!

Just last week, Toshi and her mom were walking home when a dog came up to them. Mom liked dogs. She knew a lot about them, too.

"You shouldn't just run up to a strange dog and put your hands in his face," said Mom. "Just relax and hold your arms at your sides. Let him sniff you. See?"

Mom put her hands in her pockets and let the dog smell her clothes. Then she asked the owner if it would be all right to pet him.

The man said, "Sure, he's friendly!"

Soon Mom and the dog had made friends. "You can do it, too," Mom said.

"He still might bite me!" Toshi said. She had hid behind Mom the whole time so that dog couldn't get close to her!

One Saturday Mom had to work, and
Dad was busy with Asha, Toshi's baby
sister, who was cranky. Toshi was
helping him as much as she could.

Dad said, "We're out of milk. I have
nothing to put in Asha's bottle. I wish
there were a big girl in this house who
could help me by going down to the
corner store for some milk."

"I'm a big girl!" Toshi said. "I can help you!"

Dad gave her a hug. "I know you're a little scared to walk down there by yourself, Toshi. But it's not very far, and I'll be right here waiting for you."

So Dad gave Toshi some money and she started walking. The apartment buildings on her block looked big and scary. Soon, she couldn't see her house. Her heart was pounding in her chest.

Then Toshi heard something loud. She turned around to look. . . .

JOE'S DELI

It was a big white dog! He was
running out of his building, and he was
barking at her!

Toshi ran to the nearest tree and
climbed it as fast as she could. The dog
jumped up on the tree and kept on
barking. Toshi thought she was going
to cry.

Someone ran up next to the dog. He stopped barking and sat right down. It was a girl about the same age as Toshi. "Why don't you come down from there?" she asked.

"I can't," said Toshi.

"Why not?" asked the girl.

"Because I'm afraid of him," Toshi said, pointing down at the dog.

"You don't have to be afraid of my dog," said the girl. "And she's not a 'him,' she's a 'her.' Her name's Sugar. She's really nice. Come on down so you can pet her." The girl clipped Sugar's leash to her collar.

"Sugar is not a very scary name," thought Toshi.

She looked down at Sugar, who was standing by the tree with her tongue hanging out of her mouth. She almost looked like she was smiling up the tree.

"Does she ever bite people?" Toshi asked.

"Sugar never bites," said the girl. "She just barks. That's her way of saying 'Hello!'"

Toshi took a deep breath. Slowly she
climbed down from the tree. But she
stood right beside it—just in case she
had to climb back up again.

"Hello," she said to Sugar. Sugar
sniffed her up and down.

"Put out your hand," said the girl.
"She'll lick you."

Toshi didn't know if she wanted Sugar to lick her, but she put her hand out anyway. Sugar's tongue was wet, but it was also warm and soft.

Toshi lightly touched the top of Sugar's head. It was soft, too. "This isn't so scary," Toshi said to herself. She smiled.

"My name is Meeka," the girl said.

"I'm Toshi" said Toshi.

"I'm going to the store to get some milk for my mom," said Meeka.

"I'm going there, too!" Toshi said.

On the walk home, Meeka let Toshi hold Sugar's leash. "Where do you live?" Meeka asked. "I haven't seen you around here before."

"I'm new," Toshi said, pointing to her apartment building. They counted how many buildings there were between them. Four—not many at all!

"See you tomorrow?" Meeka asked.

"Okay," said Toshi, "see you tomorrow."

The next afternoon, Meeka came over to play in the yard at Toshi's building. "If you show me how you got all the way up in that tree yesterday," said Meeka, "I'll teach you how to jump Double Dutch. Then we can play with the big kids out front."

Toshi climbed all the way to the top of the old tree—slowly, so Meeka could see how she did it. "Just hold on tight, find a good spot for your feet—and don't look down," said Toshi. "Now you try!"

Meeka climbed up to the first big branch. Then she stopped. She held on tight—and looked down.

"What's wrong?" asked Toshi. "You're doing great!"

"I'm too scared," Meeka said. "I can't climb any higher!"

"Yes you can, Meeka! You're brave!" said Toshi. "You aren't scared of dogs. You aren't afraid to go to the store by yourself. You aren't afraid to jump rope with the big kids. You can do anything if you just try!"

Meeka held on tight. She didn't look down. She climbed until she was almost as high up in the tree as Toshi.

When Toshi's mom stuck her head out the window to call Toshi in for dinner, she saw the two girls sitting near the tippy-top of the old tree. They were laughing and cheering.

"What are you girls playing?"
called Mom.

"We're playing a new game,"
said Toshi. "It's called *The Bravest
Girls in the World!*"

▲▲▲▲▲ JUST FOR YOU ▲▲▲▲▲

Here are some fun things for you to do.

Brave, Brave YOU!

Toshi was *very* afraid of dogs. Why do you think Meeka was able to help Toshi get over her fear?

Think of a time when YOU were afraid of something. Does that something seem scary now?

How did you get over YOUR fear? Did someone help you?

Write a story about overcoming a fear. Call it: "The True Story of Brave, Brave Me!"

Name That Dog!

Think about Meeka's dog. Why do you think she named her dog Sugar?

Remember the other dog Toshi met? Make up a name for him.

Then draw a picture to show what will happen the next time Toshi meets that little dog. Will she hide or will she try to make friends? Will the dog growl or want to play?

What happens in the picture is up to YOU!

Three Up a Tree

How would YOU feel
if Toshi asked you to climb
that tree? Would you need
some help from Toshi, too?

Imagine you are there with
the girls. How would you
feel about starting to climb?
Getting halfway up?
Reaching the top?

Make up a comic strip! Show
what happens—and how
YOU feel—step by step.

▲▲▲▲TOGETHER TIME ▲▲▲▲

*Make some time to share ideas about the story with your young
reader! Here are some activities you can try. There are no right or
wrong answers!*

Talk About It: Toshi tells Meeka: "You can do anything if you
just try!" Ask your child, "How did these words help Meeka?" Why
is it important for everyone to take on new challenges? Share
your own experiences with your child, too. Talk about why almost
everyone needs help to learn new things.

Read More: This story is big on girl power! Visit the library to
find more stories about brave, adventurous girls, such as
Thunder Rose by Jerdine Nolen, *Just Like Josh Gibson* by Angela
Johnson, *Jo-Jo's Flying Side Kick* by Brian Pinkney, and *The
Moon Ring* by Randy DuBurke, the illustrator of this story!

Act It Out: What happened when Toshi got home from the
store? What might she have told her parents about Meeka and
Sugar? Let your child pretend to be Toshi. You can play Mom or
Dad. Together, act out what each character would say. And
remember to have fun!

Meet the Author

OLIVIA GEORGE says, "I had lots of fears when I was younger. As I grew up I realized that many of the things I was most afraid of were things I really wanted to do. Conquering a fear by facing it was always very exciting. It still is! I've learned that it's okay to be afraid, as long as I don't let the things I'm afraid of keep me from having new experiences, and making great new friends!"

Olivia was born and raised in Brooklyn, New York, on a block with lots of big kids and dogs. She has always loved to write, and she was lucky enough to have teachers, family members, and friends who not only encouraged her but made wonderful characters for her stories! A graduate of Princeton University in New Jersey, she now lives in Oakland, California, where she is a certified massage therapist, child-care provider, freelance editor, and full-time dreamer. This is her first book.

Meet the Artist

RANDY DuBURKE says, "I love Toshi and Meeka's friendship—the heart and soul of this story. They each have fears, but they are able to help each other overcome them and reach their full potential. Helping each other is a crucial part of any true and lasting friendship. That's something I value in my relationships."

Randy was born in Washington, Georgia, but moved to Brooklyn, New York, when he was very young. A self-taught artist, he has been drawing for as long as he can remember. Randy studied graphic design at New York City Technical College, where he received an Associate of Arts and Science degree. He has done illustration work for the *New York Times Book Review, MAD Magazine,* MTV, and DC and Marvel Comics. His first picture book, *The Moon Ring,* which he wrote and illustrated, was the winner of the Coretta Scott King/John Steptoe New Talent Award for Illustration in 2003. Randy now lives in Switzerland with his wife and son.